Miscellany of Musings

Nicole Wilkinson

BookLeaf
Publishing

Presentation by *BookLeaf Publishing*

Web: www.bookleafpub.com

E-mail: info@bookleafpub.com

ISBN: 9789357212137

First edition 2023

To all who have inspired, supported and understood my love for words and writing.

ACKNOWLEDGEMENT

Robert Browning
Dr Seuss
Oscar Wilde

PREFACE

An ad hoc activity which turned into passion.

Self Expectations

Stagnation,

Spiralling procrastination,

Struggling with indecision,

Soul searching, seeking solutions.

Sentient,

Stripped senseless,

Shackled by shame,

Self-loathing seeps settles in.
Surrender,

Start over,

Survivor, second chance,

Slow single step forward.

Sage,

Seminal moment,

Simplicity is key,

Stimulation starts strongly streaming.

Gone Astray

Numerous notations, scraps of sentences left
discarded, abandoned in a pile,

Lamentably, creative inspirations gone astray for
quite awhile.

Countless times grasping pen, scribbling away
forging a start,

Before long left utterly dispirited, unable to
fashion words into art.

Determined perseverance, refusing to concede
literary flair has passed away,

Suddenly, inexplicably first phrases then verse
began flowing once again today.

People

One of my greatest delights in life, meeting new
people and having the chance to socialize,

It constantly fascinates me given the right cue
how much people like to share and vocalize,

I avoid using stereotypes believing them
judgemental serving only to stigmatize,

However that said, many of us talk the same
language I have come to realize,

From experience I've discovered, several
personalities by which individuals can be
characterized,

Some tend towards being dramatic, reveling at
any chance to scandalize,

For others everything is open to debate, every
possibility examined till nothing remains to
scrutinize,

Not forgetting the gloomy few, seeking a
sympathetic ear as woefully they agonize,

Thankfully there aren't many I find intolerable,
other than those who lack manners and like to
patronize,

Last but not least are my favourites the witty
jokers who love to satirize.

Sea of Black

A roaring surge,

A sinister swell of black,

A maverick monstrous wave,

Mercilessly savage,
Malevolently crashing down on me.

Unrelentless,

Punishingly powerful,

Pummelling, pounding till weakened and limp,

Finally, battered and beaten,

Held captive, it's prisoner.

Battling Anxiety

Guaranteed the only absolute remaining the
same,

Inexplicably disappearing as mysteriously as
you came.

A beast impossible to capture, let alone tame,

Wreaking havoc as you destroy and maim.

We've faced off more times than I care to name,

Your mission to conquer have me crumble and
cower in shame.

Do not underestimate my courage, endurance for
this game,

No matter what, victory will never be yours to
claim.

Empty Nest

Stark is the silence in this empty nest,

Left with a hole in my heart and an ache in my chest.

Bon voyage, discovering the world your quest,

Steadfast and confident, you will meet every challenge and conquer any test.

Fearing the worst, fretfully praying unable to rest,

Finding calm by steering thoughts into activities with energetic zest.

Celebrating your return feeling contently blest,

Sharing tales of adventure, lovingly indulgent of my motherly request.

Australian Twang

Albeit a blessing, a burden, being bred with an
Australian twang,

Creating confusion many a conundrum, as a
composer of rhyme.

My beloved dictionary, advisor on what's
acceptable what's slang,

Every poem I write, assessing each word, one at
a time.

Endlessly practising pronunciation, ever anxious
to avoid critical harangue,

Perseverance pays when finally prose flows
perfectly sublime.

A Whiff of Whimsy

Kicks off with a joke, prank, or pun,

Smile slippery sliding into a smirk,

A snort becomes a snicker,

Chortle a cheeky chuckle.

A gaggle of gleeful giggles,

Generates a gigantic guffaw,

Booming boldly into a boisterous bellow,

A crackling cacophony of commotion,

Resulting in a raucous roar of rollicking rabble,

Ludicrous lunacy, loud larks and laughter,

Topsy-turvy tomfoolery joyously and playfully
tickles the soul.

The Telephone Call

Silence, slumber suddenly shattered,

Shrilling shriek of the telephone,

Shuddering, sleepily I shot upright,

Clutching clumsily to take the call,

Confused, clueless glancing at the clock.

Brazenly it blinked, boasting 4am,

Frozen with fear as to what would follow,

A familiar voice delivers devastating news,

Dazed, destroyed dropping the line,

Downwards I sunk, drowning in despair.

Lesson Learned

Allow me to be brutally honest 'shoot straight from the hip',

I will share a lesson learned, a valuable survival tip,

A simple remedy for coping when everything gives you the pip,

Avoid feeling overwhelmed, scared you may freak out and flip,

Stop what you're doing, away you must slip,

Pause for a moment, take stock get a grip,

Take time to regenerate, relax maybe enjoy a quiet kip,

Follow this advice and the challenges you face, will seem conquerable a mere blip.

Growth

God's creation,

Germination triggers gestation,

Gradation, granule into grain,

Greedily grasping sun,

Gluttonously gulping air,

Glimmer, a glimpse of green.

Fusion,

Fervently feeding,

Fertile fruition,

Fiercely forging forward,

Fulminating in a flare of fronds,

Finishing with a flamboyant floral flourish.

Why

With great sorrow, overwhelming grief,

Four anguished souls mourned and wept,

Shattered by denial, left broken in disbelief,

Final moments, painful images hard to accept.

Freed from torment, finally escaping and finding release,

Leaving for reasons I cannot fathom nor deduce,

Praying the beyond has brought stillness and peace,

Four precious lives felled, taken by a noose.

The Stare

15

Happy, fun-loving without a care,

Anger is a sentiment, seldom expressed or
shared.

The triggers for such instances are extremely
rare,

Neither attitude nor demeanor will signal a flare,

The only exception is my fiery stare.

By chance, this is the look I wear,

Forewarned, I urge stop, beware.

Finding Balance

The eternal quest seeking to balance work and
leisure,

A complicated challenge to strike the right
measure.

A creature of habit it's always been a struggle
for me,

Setting aside all tasks, letting them be.

Long has it bewildered and baffled me, I must
confess,

Given my understanding of the consequences of
stress.

Despite best intentions again I fall prey to
relapse,

Slavishly toiling until exhaustedly I collapse.

Recovering from the grind, after another
punishing fight,

Finally, realising why consistently I'd failed to
get the harmony right.

Industriously diligent, words by which I've
always been described,

Laudable traits of personality, supposedly I've
been ascribed.

A sentiment with which generally I concur, I do
say,

However only when applied wisely and in the
most careful way.

Second nature its become, always the purveyor
of good deeds,

Take stock, learn from me, the terrible toll of
sacrificing your own needs.

Hot Summers Day

The working day over home at long last,

The frenzy to meet deadlines, all over and in the past,

The day quickly turned to night, the sun sinking fast,

I rushed inside to escape another day of sweltering heat,

Strangely concerning was the unsettling silence that I did meet,

Rather than the usual thundering of excited bounding feet,

I sped out to the garden filled with panicked dismay,

Spotting a familiar form I sighed, all fears draining away,

Shaded under the trees there she lifelessly lay,

Filling her bowl I rushed to her fast,

In a frenzy of slurping, she drank not pausing a beat,

With every drop gone, she lay down cool at last,

Eventually, after a moment she rose to her feet,

Wagging her tail barking excitedly her happy 'good day',

Companionably we went inside, out of the summer heat.

The Storm

Streaking bolts of light flash the cloudy sky,

In the distance, it begins softly but recognisably distinct.

Frighteningly faint the menacing murmurs gather momentum,

As I listen, the rumbles rise rapidly to a raucous, rebellious roar.

Eyes squeezed tightly shut,

Shaky hands clamped covering my ears.

Bracing against the cacophony of every clanging rattle,

Cowering as the crescendo of furious clatter peaks.

Rages shrieking to a climax, crashing with a bang of booming clapping.

Composing myself, drawing a deep shuddery
breath,

Seemingly an eternity had passed.

Summoning the courage quickly counting to ten,

Cold clammy hands withdrawn from ears, eyes
blink open.

Desperately hoping the wild weather has
subsided,

A peaceful stillness has come to pass.

Whilst silence did not greet me, a soothing
sound did prevail,

A steady streaming pitter-patter of splashing,
swirling, spluttering and spattering.

Quake

22

Fault displacement, tectonic breaks,

Seismic waves vibrate and rumble,

Amplitude intensifies in a seizure of shocks and shakes,

Magnitude climaxes, crashing into a pile of crumble.

A seemingly endless avalanche of tremors and quakes,

Spasms finally slow, stopping with a groan and a grumble,

Emerging from shelter, life moves and awakes,

Sights of destruction, devastate, and humble.

You

Gone you left me here,

Heartbroken wishing you were near.

Ever after that day secretly haunted by fear,

Growing stronger with the passing of each year.

Since then spending hours staring off into space,

Desperate to capture and remember your face.

A vivid image of you I struggle to embrace,

As I dreaded, nothing but blankness in its place

Who Defines Me

I am who I am and so uniquely me,

The influence of two important people played key.

My charming, witty charisma inherited from my beloved mother,

My love of challenging adventure, inspired by my courageous brother.

Clouds

25

My eyes staring way up high,

Gazing trancelike at the sky,

Perfect way to allow time to pass by.

More than shades of black and blue,

Always bringing something new,

Infinite colours, every hue.

Sights of delight numerous,

Blue, white and voluminous,

Soft, ethereal cumulus.

Lockdown

Waiting for word to come down the wire,

Alert, growing agitated and feeling increasingly anxious.

Any moment another announcement will be made,

In the interim, the press postulates a plethora of predictions.

After much time has ticked by,

Miraculously our Leader materializes.

Purposefully powering to position himself at the podium,

Tonelessly talking, he delivers a devastating dialogue.

Detailing the direction we will take to defeat the deadly virus spreading,

Lockdown, leaving home limited to essential
errands.

Stay safe by social distancing and sanitizing,

Mask-wearing will be mandatory.

Respect the restrictions and take care,

Together we will fight the vicious and virulent
virus.